DECIDE

THERE'S USUALLY A CHOICE. IT'S USUALLY YOURS.

BRADLEY CHARBONNEAU

REPOSSIBLE

For my Mom

Because at some point early on in my childhood she instilled in me the idea that who I would become was a choice and that choice was up to me.

PREFACE

"I didn't have time to write a short letter, so I wrote a long one instead."

— MARK TWAIN

I read a really long book recently and there were 14 different topics.

I forgot what most of them were.

The few I did remember were less solid because they were bogged down by the others I forgot about.

I'm shooting for a single topic and we can cover it succinctly and quickly.

I think it can be done and I'm going to do it. My strategy is to create shorter books with, ideally, one topic per book.

That's my decision.

See?

I've already made one.

It's going to make writing—and reading—this book easier, more efficient, and more effective.

And we're only in the Preface.

CONTENTS

PROLOGUE

"My drummer, bass player, and guitar player sing backgrounds.
They play and sing. I can sing all the harmonies, but I can't do it
alone."

— AARON NEVILLE

*I*f you're reading this, you've already made a decision.
Several, actually.

1. To see the cover,
2. Think about your challenges,
3. Buy this book,
4. Open it up,
5. Read this page.

That's already 5 decisions. We're only in the Prologue.
**There's another decision that might change this book,
future books, and your perspective on the future.**
That might seem like a lot, but I'm asking, yep, early on in this

book, to think about questions you have as you read, feedback, improvements, and your own opinion.

I'm seeking your feedback, comments that are only yours, ideas that might be hiding under the surface, experiences unique to you, case studies—anything that will make the book better for future readers who could benefit from the goodness that you'll (hopefully!) find inside these pages.

The stories in this book are mostly mine. That's fine and all, but they will be better if this book becomes "ours" instead of just "mine" or seen from your perspective, "his."

In return, I'll share early editions of my upcoming books, provide you with free or discounted rates, and, on your deathbed, you'll receive total consciousness.

(OK, 2 out of 3 isn't bad, right?)

Up for it?

Check out the following URL for extras, video, audio, and whatever else you and we can dream up to add even more value to the power of *Decide*.

decide.repossible.com

Without you, it's just me. Without you I'm just I. But with you, we're we and not just from my perspective, but from yours as well. I invite you to make this "we" instead of "me."

FOREWORD

There are 71 questions in this book. Bradley Charbonneau asks a lot of questions.

Along the way he also asked me to write this foreword to his latest book, *Decide, There's Usually a Choice. It's Usually Yours.* So I guess that makes 72 questions.

The reward for asking a lot of questions is people often decide to say yes to something you want. I decided to say yes for a ton of reasons, mostly for the joy of helping Bradley and some for the fun of telling parts of his story that he doesn't. A little bit risky on his part, if you ask me! Like asking the friend you'd spent a weekend in Vegas with to give a toast at your wedding.

Bradley is by far the most curious person I've ever met and having a curious friend means every conversation is an adventure.

For this author, every adventure is also a potential topic for his Every Single Day (ESD) habit of writing, now at day #2,165. Which is close to six years!

I don't know about you, but there aren't very many things beyond basic hygiene and sustenance I've done every single day for six years!

I met Bradley on #910 ESD. Within a few hours of meeting him

I bluntly stated, "You will get me to write." Only a little pressure on my brand new acquaintance!

Turns out encouraging people to develop a writing habit, write books with their kids, and all things around creating and marketing books, only adds fuel to Bradley's Eternal Flame Falls.

In between discovering Charlie Holiday's superpowers and chasing lost balls through castles and caverns, Bradley supports writers with podcasts, and courses such as *Audio for Authors* and *How to Publish Your First Book*.

Like the *Eternal Flame Falls*, when we first met, Bradley's passion for writing was a natural gas pocket looking for a lighter. Steady fuel supplied his daily habit of writing and posting to his blogs.

He figured there were some books in there somewhere.

He had already decided he didn't want to do what he'd been doing for all those years when he was pretending he wasn't a writer.

He was open to more, confused about much, and curious about EVERYTHING. He was making those small decisions he talks about in this book. The ones that lead you closer to places you are drawn to visit, yet haven't quite decided to live.

On #912 ESD Bradley had no idea what was coming. He hadn't gotten up going, "today is the day my life changes." However, he was the one who decided in a split second to say yes to all he'd secretly been asking for.

My guess is that when he reads this foreword for the first time he will be surprised to make the connection that his exuberant decision (as in jumping up and down on the side of the road) to blurt out the words, "Hey, give it to me. I'll take it," altered the course of his life.

As Bradley writes in *Decide*, our hearts will guide us to make decisions if we trust it. He wasn't using his thinking decision making skills when he said those words, he was deciding from a place of inner knowing. A knowing that told him very quickly and clearly, "I want that!"

And with that simple decision he got more than a Bic lighter that would quickly run out of fuel, he got a lifetime supply of fireworks! When his heart exploded with electricity, sending bolts of orange, red and yellow into his body, Bradley's writing caught fire and he's never looked back.

Decide is sort of a prequel to *Every Single Day*, which documented Bradley's challenges and successes, and how his decision to write for 30 days led to #2165 ESD and counting.

Decide will always be a work in progress. Such is the joy of technology that authors can easily update their published work as more decisions lead to more questions that lead to more answers that lead to more decisions.

It's a beautiful cycle. One that encourages curiosity, allows for more, and negates the pressure to come up with the right decision.

Decide to dive in now.

Answer one, or all, of those 71 questions for yourself. Who knows what doors will open for you?

The answers you decide are true for you, may well be different from Bradley's, and that is a very good thing.

After all, it got you to Decide.

Adwynna MacKenzie
Author of Carefree, where you can read the rest of Bradley's #912 ESD story.

PART I

THINK

1

INTRODUCTION
THINK

"Procrastination is opportunity's assassin."

— VICTOR KIAM

*T*hat thing you think is going to happen might not happen.

You think it will. It probably will. No, it will. But then, it might not.

"I know it will get done at some point."

But what if it never gets done?

A few days after my father's passing, I was in his office in his house. There were stacks of paper on his desk. For some reason, those stacks of paper affected me deeply.

Although my dad was gone from the physical world, those papers did not go with him. Since my dad's passing, I am happy to say that I somehow have a lighter view on what it means to leave the physical realm of life as we know it.

Now you might be scratching your head wondering how I

jumped from papers on a desk to some sort of spiritual afterworld, but I'll connect the dots, I promise.

I'd like to think there is an administrative office in heaven where you sit down in a plush chair, are offered a Chai tea latte, and they tell you every checkbox, all of your to-do lists, and pretty much everything you ever needed to finish, have been completed.

Since this is heaven and I struggled to gather interview subjects for this research, we're going to have to go with hearsay.

Because if it's truly heaven and it lives up to all of the hype, then not only will your to-do lists and public tasks be completed, but even those dreams you had hidden deep in your heart are either done or, maybe even better, are now available for you to finish and you had all of the resources and all of the time and all of the energy you needed to make it happen.

Now that I have heaven covered, let's move back to the physical, alive realm of earth and life as we know it.

Those papers on the desk.

They're not going to complete themselves, on their own, without you, or by some heavenly administrative angel. Yeah, sorry about that.

In fact, as far as my dad taking care of those papers, I feel quite certain to state they will never get done.

Never

"Never" is one of those short, five letter words, that are hard for us to comprehend because our minds can't get a hold on something like infinity. Again, let's descend back to the world we know of finite time, of say for example, a lifetime, or next Thursday.

"Next Thursday" is the opposite of never. Next Thursday is a finite, defined deadline I just pulled out of thin air but here's the beauty of the next Thursday deadline: if I decide to get it done by that date, and I follow through on my decision, it will be done and the option for "never" is now off the table.

To delve into semantics for just a moment and combine it with simple mathematics, "someday" and "never" have the same numerical value in that they both equal zero, or in other words, they are valueless, they have no worth, it will never get done.

Decide

The difference between something getting done and something not getting done is extremely simple yet not necessarily always easy.

There is a distance between done and not done that either can be measured with a microscope or satellite imagery. In other words, the difference between done and not done is either so tiny we can't see it or so vast we can't see it either.

The difference between the two comes down to one simple, not always easy, action: decide.

Maybe my dad had decided to take care of one or some or all of the papers on his desk, but he just ran out of time.

Remember when I said I would connect the dots? This is that moment.

Although we have the power to make a decision today, that does not equate to accomplishing what we decide, it only means we have chosen our path and we have taken the first step.

However, let me be clear, by making a decision to go forward at least opens up the opportunity for success whereas by not deciding or, of course, deciding not to do something, the statistical probability of achieving that thing is down to a big, fat, simple to understand zero.

In simple mathematics, the difference between zero and any other number, be it one or 427, is the same.

The difference being the same as the difference between yes or no, done or not done, alive or dead.

Putting aside momentarily the angelic staff of administrative superheroes, we have one power on this earth that is potentially our greatest strength as humans.

That power is to decide.

2

OOPS, THAT'S ONE DECISION ALREADY
DIDN'T EVEN NOTICE, DID YOU?

"The most difficult thing is the decision to act, the rest is merely tenacity. The fears are paper tigers. You can do anything you decide to do. You can act to change and control your life; and the procedure, the process is its own reward."

— AMELIA EARHART

There are several arrows on the cover of this book.

On an earlier design of the cover, there were four arrows, one of the arrows was facing down or back or in reverse or returning or giving up or whatever negative label we'd like to give it.

However, and I might add this is part of the mysterious, secretive, and powerful spell that decisions have on us, because you looked at the image, the graphic, the arrows and thought about it for a split second, wondered what they meant, deciphered and translated and interpreted your own meaning of where those arrows were going and what direction they were going in, that is already a decision past zero.

Just the tiniest of thoughts, a beginning, a forming, a seed of an idea is already one step in the direction in the decision-making process.

Because you saw this book, because you even glanced at it, because your brain analyzed the arrows and thought about them, there is no turning back. Now the decision has you under its spell.

I'm trying not to say this in a threatening manner, but more of one of respect. Respect for the power of the decision. That we are conscious of the hundreds or thousands of tiny decisions that constantly alter the trajectory on a second by second, minute by minute, and day by day basis, all the time, every year, throughout our lives.

As I write this, I completely realize it may seem daunting, it may seem like a huge dark cloud weighing upon us.

But this is where we turn things around.

This is where we climb up through that huge dark cloud, scramble up through the damp cotton ball world, rise up to where things are lighter, fluffier, and drier.

We arrive at the point where we are on top of that cloud, where we use it as a trampoline but don't bounce around haphazardly like a toddler, but rather use the exponential power because as we are conscious of our thoughts, ideas, and decisions, they begin to work for us.

No longer is the weight of decisions heavy on our shoulders, but rather it becomes the spring in our step.

There is no arrow facing downward.

There is no return from this point.

You cannot unsee the image of the three arrows for they are now ingrained in your mind forever.

Having this information, knowing that there now is no way back, you tighten the laces on your shoes, you lift your chin up, and look forward towards your next decision.

3

A SMIDGEN OF A GLANCE AT THE SEED OF A THOUGHT

WELL, THAT SEEMS INSIGNIFICANT.

"Often, little situations trigger enormous reactions. Be there, present for it. Your partner will find it easier to see it in you, and you will find it easier to see it in them."

— ECKHART TOLLE

A billboard. A bird. A wink from a stranger. What that woman said in the film last night. The touch of his hand on your shoulder. A book.

Something triggered the first thought. A tiny little speck of almost nothingness caused the beginning of something that sent the next thing into action which rolled into that part and finally ended up as that thing.

Can we trace it all back?

Did you move to Spain because your aunt Penelope said her cousin bought a sombrero and even though that's Mexican and not Spanish her cousin told you a story about her friend who lives in Valencia and introduced you? Then three years later you were married to the friend's accountant?

All from a sombrero?

A smidgen of a glance at the seed of a thought.

They happen all the time. Which ones stick? Which ones fizzle out? Which ones cannot be stopped even if you wanted them to?

Are they under our control? If so, how much? A little? All control? I doubt it.

How much are we involved? Is it fate or do we have a choice in the matter?

The sombrero? Seriously?

Watch out for what triggers the slightest trajectory change in your decision-making process.

Listen to aunt Penelope.

You never know where things might lead.

4

NOT SIMPLE AND NOT EASY

LET'S MAKE IT ALL REALLY COMPLICATED

"Life is really simple, but we insist on making it complicated."

— CONFUCIUS

Just in case things went too quickly for you back in the introduction, let's make sure we've checked all of the boxes to get rolling.

1. Not Simple
2. Not Easy

This is a good place to start so it will get better as we go along.

Not Simple

We have a lot to cover in this book. Tons. Maybe we should make it a 3-volume set. Let's call it Complex. Complicated. Rocket Science.

We might need a follow-up workshop (complete with really long workbook) to run through all of the steps. Maybe we need an app, too. Apps are great. Yes, we need more apps.

OK, sorry. Let me get back to not simple.

This is a big decision we're up against. We're up against the decision to, well, make more decisions.

"Because it's difficult, it must be complex."

— SOMEONE PROBABLY SAID

Let's go with weight loss. Simple, right? Lose weight!

Slow down there, Pendergrass. We need to learn about nutrition and our diet, do tests to test our sugar levels and how many carbs we should balance with our proteins. What are proteins, anyway? Let's take a course at the local college. That should take a semester. Then we'll start on the diet.

Complicated.

Good. Have we covered that well enough? Let's move on to even worse things.

Not Easy

We just learned we have loads to do and it's going to take a long time. That can't be fun. That can't be easy. Let's make sure we have it all lined up. I smell a numbered list coming …

1. **Checkboxes:** we're going to need lots of lists to check off what we're doing. It might help tone down the Not Simple a little if we have multiple, categorized, color-coded lists.
2. **Time:** did you sign up for the course on nutrition yet? I'm not even sure they're open for enrollment until the next semester.
3. **Peers:** tell our friends and family or not tell our friends and family? If we do we'll have some accountability.

That could get ugly. If we keep it to ourselves and then only go public when we've made some progress we'll be a success story and it will be easier to talk about.

4. **Mindset:** we can't forget that we need to make this Not Easy so we're convinced it will work. If it were too simple and too easy, it certainly wouldn't work. I mean, right? Mindset shift: this is Not Easy.

That seems complicated enough.

Action Steps

1. Get going on the list building.
2. Buy colored pencils. Or maybe pens. Whatever is erasable.
3. Sign up for college course on nutrition.
4. Tell friends. Or don't.
5. Change my mindset to make sure I know it's going to be Not Simple and Not Easy.

No, the Real Action Steps

1. Don't do any of the above action steps.
2. Keep reading.
3. Get a cup of tea or coffee.

We'll get past this.

5

WHAT WAS THAT TINGLE IN THE HAIRS ON THE BACK OF YOUR NECK?

IT MIGHT BE THE SOMBRERO

"If I don't get the goose-bump factor when I'm reading it then I can't do it."

— RUSSELL CROWE

Just as you're doubting the whole sombrero escapade, the hairs on the back of your neck start to tingle.

I could throw loads of science your way backing up the numbers behind the decision-making trajectory and possibly wow you with all kinds of theories and books and research.

Or the hairs on the back of your neck could stand up.

I'm all for science. I'm a numbers guy, a math lover, a guy who often reads the manual.

But then comes along gut feeling.

When you just know. Or at least it feels like something is right (or wrong). It's not provable, you can't necessarily share the why or what or how, but it's just there.

I say this way too often in my books, but you can skip the rest of the chapters and go with this one if you'd like. That gut feeling? Those hairs on your neck? Goosebumps?

To me, those are the indicators that defy logic. The telltale signs of something larger at play.

I'm not saying you have to believe me. I'm only asking that you keep an open mind.

The next time you have that feeling—and you know what it is, however it comes your way—take note of it.

Take a moment and think about whatever it was that you just did that caused something in your body to do something.

Our own power of thought is something many of us underestimate or even take for granted. All we did was create a thought and it caused a physical reaction in our physical body.

When else does that happen?

If we're scared, we might flinch. If we're sad, we might cry.

But here, something is triggered and it's causing a physical reaction. Are they not the same thing?

The power of our own thoughts is something we can use to our advantage.

Take that confidence, that feeling of goodness and hold onto it because we're about to head into the section of the book called doubt.

PART II

DOUBT

6

INTRODUCTION
DOUBT

"Procrastination is one of the most common and deadliest of diseases and its toll on success and happiness is heavy."

— WAYNE GRETZKY

I realize we just finished the section that ended with happy places like sombreros and hairs tingling on your neck.

I daresay that this section titled "Doubt" is optional, but I'm going to say it anyway. It's optional.

"But I like doubt! Doubt gives me freedom from deciding and doesn't force me to move forward! It's a cozy, friendly place where I can hang out forever!"

— BRADLEY CHARBONNEAU (NOT THE AUTHOR OF THIS BOOK, BUT ANOTHER BRADLEY CLEARLY)

I mostly want to give you the out, the chance, the right to make doubt optional. Let me put it this way: I used to believe doubt wasn't optional. In fact, it was a clear link in the chain of the whole, really long, cumbersome process.

Let me skip ahead a few chapters: it's optional.

We don't need to doubt.

Sure, we can analyze and weigh the pros and cons, but the doubt I'm referring to is more of the sombrero and neck hair variety. It's the kind we don't need to, well, doubt.

With that, if you'd like to trudge along knee-deep in the morass of swampy doubt, let's get started.

7

THE SCHOOL UNIFORM AND UNLEASHING MASSIVE BRAIN POWER

LET'S SEE, HOW ABOUT THE WHITE BUTTON DOWN AND THE KHAKI PANTS TODAY?

"Creativity is piercing the mundane to find the marvelous."

— BILL MOYERS

Unless you're a kid and go to a school where they require you to wear the same exact uniform to school every single day, you have a decision to make on a morning-by-morning basis.

Those kids, however much they dislike the white polo shirt and khaki pants for the boys and a pleated long skirt for the girls, have one pretty big decision less to make every morning.

They don't even think about it anymore.

It's now ingrained in them to not make a decision because that decision was made for them and will be made for them as long as they're at that school.

Each morning there is free space in their brains for different, better, hopefully bigger decisions.

That free space will make those other decisions easier.

Let's do a little math.

1. School uniform
2. Breakfast
3. Brain power jet fuel

$1 + 2 < 3$

One plus two is less than three.

Did you catch that little bonus in there? Because no energy was expended on #1 and there's left over energy for #2, there is even more energy left for the post-#2 decisions of the day.

#1 is done

#2 is easier

#3 is extra brain power

Anything beyond #2 (e.g. #3, #4, #5, etc.) is better, easier, and double bonus brownie points: even *stronger* each day.

As we make decisions, even the smallest of them, our brain gets better at it. It's a muscle. If we exercise it, it can get stronger.

It also realizes very soon when it doesn't have to make the #1 decision and can more quickly get to #2.

TIP: What could we do for the #2 decision of the day to make that a non-decision as well (if applicable). Pretty soon our breakfast-choice decision-making will be something measured in nanoseconds.

Can you see where this is going?

After breakfast you'll be solving the economic crisis in Greece. By lunch, you'll have so much extra brain power you'll be hot on the trail of a new cure for cancer.

As your decision-making expertise grows, even the bigger decisions will become easier.

Ah, the day when you look back and sigh at the energy and neurons you spent agonizing over the beige socks or the brown socks. How many hours of your life did you scuttle away?

If the school uniform doesn't do it for you, let's list just a few that might get your attention:

1. Lose weight
2. Stop smoking
3. Quit job

Doubtful? We are still in the section of this book called "Doubt," after all.

If every single morning, you didn't have to decide whether or not you were going to continue on your weight loss regimen, you would have that much more room in your mind to, for example, think about new ways to make it happen faster.

Fashion note: this is not to say that wearing the same thing for the rest of your life is a good idea. In fact, as we'll dig into later, there are some decisions on a regular basis that are fun--or can turn into fun as we get better at making decisions in general.

8

LET'S DECIDE THIS BETTER TOGETHER
ASK ME WHAT I THINK YOU SHOULD DO

"Every question is a hypothetical question for everyone but the person who asks it."

— DAN SAVAGE

Compared to the relatively simple example of the school uniform, many decisions are not solely ours to make.

This might fall into the topic of another one-word verb book of mine, Ask, but let's for a minute think about those decisions that are possibly out of your own decision-making power.

When you're in doubt and you'd like the feedback from others, be selective in where you seek that help.

There's really only one rule when asking others about your decision:

Do they have your best interest at heart?

I love the oxygen mask in the airplane metaphor. Yep, you want to save your child next to you when there's no oxygen in the plane.

The quick and doubtful decision might be to get her the oxygen.

But then you die.

Then, well, there are about a zillion circumstances here at play in my imaginary (and terribly distressing!) example, but let's go with it as we've come this far.

But the longer-term decision is for you to take the oxygen first. Then you can:

- Care for yourself.
- Better care for the child.
- Both survive.

I'm all about collaboration and cooperation, but is asking others the best route? Be selective, be cautious, gauge whether or not your best interest is in their heart.

Ideally, you'll be better together.

9

THE TINY LITTLE SECRET OF THE TIPPING POINT

A LITTLE MORE, A LITTLE LESS.

"I don't think anyone, until their soul leaves their body, is past the point of no return."

— TOM HIDDLESTON

There's a fear among non-decision makers that a tipping point comes along that's so big it might knock us over.

The secret of the tipping point is that we are constantly at a point of tipping.

Sure, there are bigger decisions and smaller ones, medium-sized ones and a few doozies.

But each point is a tipping point.

Each point leads to the next one and that then is the next tipping point. Which, guess what? Leads to the next one.

The trick, the art, the secret of these tipping points is to keep them small, to keep them active, and to be tipping them all the time so we become used to them and they're no longer big and scary.

More fulfilled, less fulfilled. More meaning, flow, satisfaction-- or less.

If each so-called tipping point, or let's tone it down a little and pull out all of the pomp and circumstance around the words, each *decision* is just a question of more fulfilled or less fulfilled, more bliss or less bliss, more gut feeling or less gut feeling, then it's easier to make that decision.

It should--and will--become as easy as a flowing river or a stick floating in that river that goes where the current is the strongest.

It's pulled a little this way, it's pushed a little that way. But it's not using any of its own energy, it's just, dare I use the pun, going with the flow.

Which is, of course, exactly the point.

As we tip, as we knock over each point along the way, just like a runner who is in shape and runs at least a little bit every day, the medium runs are easier. Even the marathon is something they're prepared for. Yes, it's a big deal, but they are more ready for it, it's not a surprise, in fact, it's a welcome challenge.

As we become more experienced with tipping, we even look forward to it as we know with each tip the next one will be that much easier.

PART III

DECIDE

INTRODUCTION

DECIDE

"Because there is a law such as gravity, the universe can and will create itself from nothing."

— STEPHEN HAWKING

We're at the mountain peak.

We made it.

But now what?

Go back from where we came? Turn left? Turn right?

Or continue what we started?

We've come this far. It's time to go through with it.

Let's say it's winter and we have a snowball in our hands. We're at the top of the mountain. We can walk it down and hold it in our hands back the way we came. Maybe toss it off to the left or right.

Or send it on its way straight ahead. Let it head down the hill. Gain momentum. Build up speed. Get bigger and bigger.

Soon, there will be no stopping it.

Because we have reached the midpoint of this book and we have decided.

There's no turning back now.

OK, fine, you can turn back. You can stop reading, I suppose. But then I should write a follow-up book called, "Undecided: It was my choice. I didn't do it."

Let's head to the field of dreams.

11

DECIDE AND PEOPLE WILL COME

IF YOU DON'T, THEY WON'T

"People will come, Ray. People will most definitely come."

— JAMES EARL JONES AS TERENCE MANN

(FROM FIELD OF DREAMS)

Math. I have to go back to math.

If my 14-year-old son ever reads this, he'll cringe at the thought of my bringing up math yet again in my work.

Maybe if he reads a little later, like when he's 34, he'll understand that math can be the great explainer.

Zero.

It doesn't really exist. It's nothing. It's not yet something.

The quote above is from the film Field of Dreams and the main character is debating creating a baseball field in the middle of a cornfield in Iowa.

One.

One exists. It's a real number. It's just one more than zero, but remember, zero doesn't exist.

If he doesn't build the baseball diamond, by definition, no one will come, no one will visit it because it doesn't exist.

If he does build it at least there's a chance people will come.

Now Terence Mann seems pretty convinced people will come. But then again, they're talking about baseball and cornfields and Iowa.

In this book, we're talking about your decisions, your plans, your dreams, your life.

If you decide, will they come?

In case that little math above didn't put you on the edge of your seat just begging for more numbers, here's the statistical probability of something happening if you do not decide:

Zero.

We're back to zero. Zero chance, zero nothing, zero nada.

If you decide, will they come?

There's no guarantee, but now there's a chance.

Here's how I see it. If you decide, they will be *swayed.*

They will respect your decision (whether they admit it openly or not for whatever reasons).

If you stick with your decision, at some point, they have to respect that you made the decision and stuck with it.

If you succeed in making the decision and then sticking with the decision and then following through and succeeding (however success might be interpreted), in my humble opinion, people will respect that.

Am I just seeking respect?

Yes.

But not from others. I care less about what they think—although I do care.

No, I'm seeking *self-respect.*

When I make the decision and keep it and follow through and make it happen, I have self-respect.

No one can take that from me. Ever. It's mine and I'm not giving it up. It's tight in my fist and no one, no one can rip it out of my fingers.

It's mine.

It's yours.

Keep it.

Decide.

12

SIMPLE BUT NOT EASY
WE'RE ALMOST THERE

"A song that sounds simple is just not that easy to write. One of the objectives of this record was to try and write melodies that continue to resonate."

— SHERYL CROW

There was a radio show called Car Talk where two guys (Click and Clack, the Tappet Brothers) talked about car repair.

I know, sounds really boring (unless you're really into car repair). But the guys were hilarious. People flocked to the show even if they cared nothing for cars.

They had off-the-wall solutions for most things (e.g. don't replace the car, replace your husband) and laughed throughout most of the program.

I searched and couldn't find an exact quote, but they had an episode where they talked about how simple it was to replace a car engine. Here are the steps. I remember them clearly because they were so simple.

PART IV

FLOW

14

INTRODUCTION

FLOW

"I just go with the flow, I follow the yellow brick road. I don't know where it's going to lead me, but I follow it."

— GRACE JONES

We're heading down the mountain. The snowball is building in speed and size. We have momentum. Not only is it difficult to turn back, we no longer want to.

We've made the decision.

Now it's time to reap the glory.

We just need to keep it going. Stick with it. Persevere. Be patient.

If others are falling away around you, it's OK. In fact, it might even be seen as a good sign: you're on your path anyway, not theirs.

Here we go.

Hold on.

15

DECISIONS BEGET DECISIONS
SHE DID THAT SO WE DID THIS WHICH LED TO THEM MAKING THAT HAPPEN

"The process of writing is like creating a game of dominoes: The first domino creates the second incident, and so forth until the end."

— ASGHAR FARHADI

My mom moved. After 49 years in the same house. I went out there and spent two weeks, 8-10 hours per day, sifting through 49 years of stuff.

beget: to cause; produce as an effect

We're renovating our house here in The Netherlands. We have to move out for 10 weeks. We're in a little "vacation house" in this "vacation park" in the woods where City Folk come to get away from it all. It's cute, it's quiet, it's small. From the moving truck that went to my wife's mom's cellar, we took only suitcases and a few things. Even too many small few things.

Last week the papers were signed and we sold an investment

property we had in California. A few years ago, it would have been a huge deal, a monumental decision, but we now just did it.

Decisions Beget Decisions

My mom decided to move. We decided to renovate. We decided to sell our house.

They influence each other. Each one made the next one easier. Note that they weren't even our own decisions, we were influenced, intrigued, and inspired by the decisions of others.

My sister now said that she ...

See how it works?

Just as we are influenced by actions, behaviors, thoughts, moods or others (and ourselves), we are influenced by the decisions and the decision-making power of others.

We can get better at making decisions. We will learn that not making a decision is actually a decision. That stalling, whining, procrastinating is really just costing us time, energy, and probably money.

Start with small ones. Work up to bigger ones. Talk to people who made the big ones. Ask them about them. How did it make them feel? What were the pros and cons? How could you learn from their decisions to make your own? How can we learn from our own decisions--and lack thereof--to make better ones from here on out?

It's like a muscle and we can work it, use it, train it, and get smarter about it.

16

THE BIG DECISIONS WILL HELP GUIDE THE SMALLER DECISIONS

THE RIVER WILL FIND A WAY

"But the rule seems to be that the bigger and more life-changing the decision, the less it will seem like a decision at all."

— HUGH MACKAY

Throughout this book, we've hopefully hammered home how important the smaller decisions are. Make lots of little decisions on a regular basis (pretty much all the time) and the bigger ones will be easier, more clear, and even light and fun.

But what about those big ones?

The career change, the move cities or countries, the have kids or not? They exist, we can't deny them. Those decisions have to be made at some point. Yes, it's true, they are easier as the smaller ones are made.

I hope it hasn't felt as if I've been hiding the big ones and in anticipation it's been a worry along the way when we're going to be dealing with them. In other words, sure, you're running around the block every day, but when are you really going to tackle the marathon?

Let's let the cat out of the bag: we need to make the big decisions, too.

Here's the exciting news: when you make the big ones, the smaller ones become even easier. Yes, we've discussed how easy the small ones can be, but when you make the big ones, the smaller ones are dessert, fun, light, and like popping a bonbon in your mouth--pure delight.

Here's the scary news: yes, we have to make them.

How to prepare for them? How to actually make them happen? How to not mess up the big one so the little ones are not messed up too?

Practice.

Build up to them. Work on the small ones, then some medium ones, then the big ones will be easier.

Let's go back to our friend the river. As the tributaries lead into the main flow, the big river, it becomes more powerful. The direction of that big river becomes easier as it's flowing faster and stronger. It arrives at the big rocks, maybe even the mountain and it might plow straight into it. Maybe the mountain breaks apart under the pressure. Maybe the river goes left. Maybe it goes right.

It's going to go where the resistance is the least.

This doesn't mean it's easiest path and not the right path. It's the path, at least in the river example, where the resistance to holding back is the least strong.

In our human being example, with our now-more-experienced-decision-making minds, it's the path that feels right, that's natural, that causes the least friction, that our gut tells us is right, that our experience in decision making points us towards.

You can't decide whether or not to upgrade your house alarm system.

Or, let's take a few more from real life:

1. Do you fix the hole in the floor in the office?
2. What to do with that old (but beautiful) Chinese chest?
3. Renew the expensive cable bill?
4. Finally replace that microwave?
5. Stocks or real estate?

These are real decisions. Many of them aren't that big, but when they're in front of you (sort of like the guy with the knife in the alley, even though, in hindsight, he was short and possibly blind and potentially asleep ...), they were Big Decisions when you were trying to make them.

Which brings us to subjective and objective decision making.

With the six decisions to be made above (including the alarm system), what if they could all be answered, solved, just plain made to vanish with a single swoosh of the magic wand?

What if you just **Know What You Need to Do**? Just all of the sudden? As if a little fairy on your shoulder told you?

Here's how.

Think bigger. Think higher. Above, beyond, longer term.

However you want to see it.

Here's what happened.

A certain someone had all of the above decisions to make. They weren't weighing down her daily life, but they were still on her mind. Occasionally, they were annoying. It would have been nice if they went away.

Then one day, possibly (no, probably) partly related to those decisions weighing down on her for weeks (if not months or years), she had a moment of clarity that would demote all of those decisions (and many, many more) from primary to secondary.

She decided it was time to move.

Move houses. Move out from where the hole in the office was. Move to a place where the Chinese chest (yes, she'd had it in the family for decades) had no place. Where cable TV was included. An alarm system built in. A microwave built after 1974 was already in the kitchen.

No longer were these decisions even on the table. They were gone. They were answered. They vanished into thin air. Just like that.

Because she thought bigger and made a larger, much more important decision.

As if the previously large decisions were buoys floating in the ocean (hard to collect, bobbing up and down, but clearly visible) and the big, new decision was the fishing boat that came through and just swept all of the buoys up and away.

Just like that, all of those decisions that used to weigh you down were now done. Answered.

Like magic.

17

WHEN YOU CHANGE YOUR MIND, YOU CHANGE YOUR MIND
NEURONS AND STUFF

"In the brain, you have connections between the neurons called synapses, and they can change. All your knowledge is stored in those synapses."

— GEOFFREY HINTON

It's not just a thought, matter changes form when you make a decision.

In case my witty play on words didn't make complete sense, let me explain what I'm getting at:

When you (1) change your mind, that is, when you make a decision, you (2) change your mind, that is, you alter the chemistry of your brain.

There are of course varying levels of how much happens, but it happens. Even when you're driving and you decide to go left instead of right, there is so much activity in your brain and part of it sticks.

If something changes in your brain with such a simple decision, can you imagine how much transforms when you make a big decision?

*Decisions--and changes in brain neurons--are relative
and subjective.*

In other words, what might seem a small decision to some
(your decision to stop eating sugar for a month) is huge to others.
But what matters most is how much it matters to you, how much it
changes how your neurons are firing, what is connecting with
what in your brain, what sticks, and what gets altered.

When you make a decision, you change your mind, you alter
your brain.

Are you ready to change your mind? Think it wasn't possible?
Change your mind, change your brain, alter your neurons.

- Change more of them.
- Do it on a regular basis.
- Get better at it.
- Get in "decision making" shape where it becomes easier
  and easier to make them.
- Get stronger with them.
- Make bigger ones.
- Change your mind.
- Change your brain.
- Change your habits.
- Change your life.

Oh, one more thing.
It works both ways.
Notice I haven't talked about success or better or even worse.
Because it can go both ways. You can make more bad decisions.
You can alter your mind for the worse just as easily as for the
better.

See how you have the power? See how there's risk, danger, but
also opportunity?

Want to know the best part?

It's up to you.

Are you going to change your mind today?

Here's my bet: having read this today, you already have.

PART V

PLAY

18

INTRODUCTION
PLAY

"Play is often talked about as if it were a relief from serious learning. But for children play is serious learning. Play is really the work of childhood."

— FRED ROGERS

*I*f you thought flow was fun, this is going to be an extra special treat.

There comes a time when you've done something for a while when you are convinced so clearly and purely that you no longer remember or recognize (or maybe it's just that you no longer care) about how you started or where you began.

We're deep in flow. We have momentum, confidence, and passion. We have long since made our decision.

Now we get to the unexpected benefits that come with decision making.

Play.

19

GIVE A VOICE TO YOUR TRUTH AND A TRUTH TO YOUR VOICE

IT'S TIME TO SPEAK UP

"There is but one cause of human failure. And that is man's lack of faith in his true Self."

— WILLIAM JAMES

Unblock the dam and let the river flow as it was meant to. We all have an inner voice or we can call it our subconscious self or it's actually fine to call it or relate to it however you want. But I think something is there, something is in there and when we are connected with it, when we are aligned with it, following it, allowing ourselves to be pulled by it, then things are easier, more meaningful, and, dare I say, effortless.

Not just effortless in that it doesn't cost us any energy, but it's actually on the other side of the neutral line from negative--it's positive. It provides energy.

Whereas when we fight it, when we push back, when we deny and avoid and pretend it isn't there, maybe never was there--when we know full well it is there, was there, and will continue to be there--we're just delaying the pain, the regret, the, dare I say, the lie.

Maybe I'm wrong.

Do you remember in school when we learned about water and how it will find a way? It will get through the mountain or around it or under it. It might build up and finally burst in a flood. Or it will trickle through the soil and create underground rivers and caverns. It's not in any big hurry. It will get there. It's also fine to wait. It will prevail.

It can also take on other forms. It can freeze while inside of a rock and break that formidable foe slowly and surely. Or it might evaporate and go above the mountain only to rain down on the other side.

See how it's not going to give up? It's going to get there. No matter what.

This is how I see our truth.

If the word truth isn't doing it for you, let's think of a few other ways to say it:

- Your true self
- Who you really are
- Who you know you are but don't want to admit
- Your passion (kinda cheesy, I admit)
- Your love
- Your truth

By giving a voice to your truth, you'll be admitting, accepting, and, ideally, embracing that this voice is yours.

How do you know what your truth is? It's easy. In fact, it's not just easy to figure out, the "easy" is part of the answer, part of the roadmap to help find it.

What comes easily to you?

What, like the water, won't (let you) give up?

What gives you satisfaction?

What, when you're not doing it or being it, makes you feel unsatisfied?

Like the water, it won't go away. Ever. It might change forms (ice, steam) but it's still there.

My thinking is then to decide to give into it, to allow it, to surrender to it, to accept it, to embrace it even.

It's a conscious decision. Your truth is there, you probably know what it is. But to decide to allow it is a moment in your life when things, most things, maybe all things, will then be set free.

They will flow.

They will find their way.

More easily.

Like the river.

When you decide to give a voice to your truth.

20

WHY DON'T THEY TEACH THIS IN SCHOOL? OR ANYWHERE?

OR MAYBE I JUST MISSED THAT DAY

"You gain strength, courage, and confidence by every experience in which you really stop to look fear in the face. You are able to say to yourself, 'I lived through this horror. I can take the next thing that comes along.'"

— ELEANOR ROOSEVELT

Maybe because I'm no longer 17 or 23 or one of those times in your life when you're pretty sure you know everything, don't need anyone to teach you anything else, and wonder why the world doesn't know what you know, but now I feel, again, like I'm 23.

Like I have the answers—or at least some of them.

As I continue to do, to write, to experience, to weigh, to ask, to answer, and to discover, I find that we can have our cake and eat it too.

We might have to bake it. It might be undercooked. The frosting might be frumpy or runny but we can have our cake and eat it too.

I suppose if I knew what I knew now when I was 17 or 23 (or 33 ...), I wouldn't be right for that age.

Do we learn what we need to learn when we need to learn it? When the time is right? When it's appropriate?

I don't believe in holding back knowledge. I want to share everything I know if it can make someone's life better or easier or more of whatever it is they're after.

Maybe they don't teach decision making in school. But if you've learned anything about it in this book, please pass it along to someone who's 17 or 23 or at least ... thinks they are.

21

WHEN ARE DECISIONS TRIGGERED IN THE SUBCONSCIOUS MINDS OF CHILDREN?

MEMORIES WITH EMOTION

"A strong emotion, especially if experienced for the first time, leaves a vivid memory of the scene where it occurred."

— ALGERNON BLACKWOOD

The good news and the bad news: they're triggered all the time.

As an adult, I'm very conscious of the fact that memories are being recorded (and tiny decisions being made) all the time in my kids--and all kids ... and all people for that matter.

The thing is: you don't know which ones are going to stick.

Or do you?

The memories with emotion are the ones that are going to stick.

You can go to a lot of trouble to make it all a big deal to try to force the memory, that important moment, but the truth is, it's going to be what it's going to be. But can we force in some emotion so it will stick?

We can try.

As much as I think it'd be wonderful if my son went to the

University of Groningen, I have little influence as to what will happen in his future. Well, I have some influence, but it's a bit like herding jellyfish: you don't want to touch them and they're just so squishy (not to mention they sting and it hurts like hell).

But some things can stick more than others.

We visited the Dutch city of Groningen for a few days and the impressions of the student town might stick in my son's mind forever.

He might remember the thump-your-heart-bass-beat of the bouncing student float. Whereas I might remember the Harry Potter-esque university building.

Then again, it might be reversed.

Who knows.

That's the beauty of the triggering of the decision-making process. We can think we have some influence, but it might go completely in another direction.

The good news? That's actually good news. If we could predict everything, what fun would that be?

22

SIMPLE AND EASY
IT'S POSSIBLE

"Happiness does not come from doing easy work but from the afterglow of satisfaction that comes after the achievement of a difficult task that demanded our best."

— THEODORE ISAAC RUBIN

*L*et's see, we've gone through:

- Not Simple and Not Easy
- Simple but Not Easy

and now we come to Simple and Easy. Could it be possible that something is both simple and easy? Wouldn't that be too good to be true?

Doesn't our hard-working upbringing tell us that it takes hard work, perseverance, and patience to get what really matters in life?

What if it weren't true?

Or at least partly untrue? Or at least a sliver of the alternative of it was possible?

Once we make the decision, the real one we're going to stick with. The one that gives us the goosebumps or makes the hairs stand up on our neck. We'll know there's no turning back.

The best way I can describe it is as a snowball.

It's simple and easy.

23

SNOWBALL

YOU MIGHT WANT TO GET OUT OF THE WAY

"People often say motivation doesn't last. Well, neither does bathing. That's why we recommend it daily."

— ZIG ZIGLAR

The "snowball effect" is what I'm going to end with. It's so appropriate on so many levels I just can't not do it.

It's simple.

It's easy.

Here's what Wikipedia has to say:

"Metaphorically, a snowball effect is a process that starts from an initial state of small significance and **builds upon itself,** becoming larger (graver, more serious), and also perhaps potentially dangerous or disastrous (a vicious circle), though it might be beneficial instead (a virtuous circle). This is a cliché in cartoons and modern theatrics and it is also used in psychology.

The common analogy is with the rolling of a snowball down a snow-covered hillside. As it rolls the ball will pick up more snow, gaining more mass and surface area, and picking up even more snow and **momentum** as it rolls along."

When you make the decision to do something, when you decide there will not be any turning back, when you know, you just know, that this is what you'll be doing for the foreseeable future, then the snowball is all you need.

Sure, you might think, "It's just frozen water. How powerful could that be?"

But it's growing, it's rolling, it's faster and getting faster. It has gravity on its side. It has momentum. It has nothing in its way except maybe the other side of the valley.

Although we have covered many aspects of decisions and the decision-making process in this book, this is the one that's most exciting.

Like a little snowball at the top of a mountain, at first it seems so innocent, so playful, so childlike.

But as it rolls down the hill and gains speed and size and weight, you quickly know there is no stopping it.

This is partly why I see this book, Decide, as the prequel to my Every Single Day book.

You need to make the snowball at the top of the hill. You need to **decide** to roll it down the mountain.

The every single day element is the rolling, the unstoppable force that the decision becomes.

Gravity. Momentum. Passion. Gut feeling. Know. Certain. Power. Ease. Play.

Snowball.

PART VI

POSTSCRIPT

24

DECIDE U.

SEE YOU IN CLASS

"When it all boils down, it's about embracing each others' stories and maybe even finding that synergy to collaborate for the common good."

— DHANI JONES

*B*ooks are awesome. Read them, cherish them, think about them, refer to them, highlight things, and … then what?

Put it on the shelf or let it drift away in the digital wasteland in the vast warehouse of your e-reader.

What if there were a place we could connect? Just a little more? Share ideas, work together, make this whole thing even better?

I've created a companion website to accompany this book where I want to share more about the decision-making process. Where we can watch videos from experts in the field. Where we can communicate with each other, ask questions, or just hang out in the back of class and listen and take notes.

In any case, a place beyond the book. Introducing:

Decide U.

To keep out the riffraff who just happen to be walking by the campus and want to come in for the lunch buffet, I'm putting a price tag on it. But as a reader of this book, we're going to waive all of that financial nonsense and let you in with a secret hall pass.

When you visit the link below to sign up, you'll be given the option of putting in a coupon code.

The coupon code below will make the price free, zero, no dollars, no Euros, no nada.

Please don't share this code with anyone who hasn't read the book as I'd like to remain a close knit group of deciders.

The coupon code is: SNOWBALL

The link to the workshop is:

decide.repossible.com

See you on campus.

25

EVERY SINGLE DAY

IT STARTS WITH THE FIRST DAY

"A dream becomes a goal when action is taken toward its achievement."

— BO BENNETT

All ready to go and don't know quite where to start? Writerly chap that I am, I suggest writing every day. It's therapeutic, meditative, and usually surprising.

I started writing because I was challenged to do so. I wasn't sure where I was heading.

Now I know.

Dare to take a first step? Or 10?

Write Every Day for 10 Days

Writing prompts, pretty pictures, directly into your email inbox. It's just 10 Days! Easy peasy, right? Spoiler alert: it might lead to more days than 10.

Head over to:

playbook.repossible.com
and sign up for free.

DID ANY PART OF THIS BOOK HELP YOU IN ANY WAY?

*Y*ou can make a huge difference in the life of someone else.

Reviews are the most powerful element when it comes to building attention for my books.

If this book, if even one chapter, helped you in any way, please remember that a simple, honest note from you about how this book helped you in a public review on the website where you bought this book, might mean that **this book will get into the hands of those who will also benefit from it.**

I would be very grateful if you could spend just a few minutes leaving a review.

It doesn't need to be long, maybe just highlight one tiny thing where it resonated with you.

Maybe the potential reader will resonate with *you*.

Thank you very much.

Bradley Charbonneau

FREQUENCY

Building a relationship with my readers is one of the best things about writing.

I occasionally send an email with details about **new books**, **sneak peeks** into Works In Progress, early bird **deals**, as well as exclusive, **Readers Only insights** into the writing and publishing process.

If you'd like to sign up to be on my Readers Only mailing list, just click on this link and let me know which email to send to. Thank you!

bradleycharbonneau.com/subscribe/

ABOUT THE AUTHOR

Bradley Charbonneau decided to become a writer when he wrote his first letter home when living abroad in France during university.

He used that thin airmail paper that's light blue and you can't read very well if you write on both sides.

But if you're paying by the gram and you suddenly have lots to write about because you find that life becomes more alive when you put it onto paper, then you use both sides.

Then that "reality" thing got in the way for many years. That whole job and house and kids and mortgages thing. So annoying. He didn't write much.

Life wasn't quite as alive.

But he decided again when someone pushed him, challenged him to start writing again.

Since that day, he hasn't stopped.

Nowadays, all he really wants to do is tell stories, travel with his wife to oddball destinations by rickety transport, shoot baskets with his boys, try to perfect the burrito outside of California, and whisper the secrets of freedom and deep joy to whomever is within earshot and shares even the slightest inkling of curiosity.

He currently lives in a little town outside of Utrecht in The Netherlands with his wife Saskia, famous two young boys of "The Adventures of Li & Lu" fame, and their at-least-as-famous dog Pepper.

This is Bradley's twelfth book.

It is far, far, far from his last.

THE END

NO, REALLY, THIS IS IT.

Thank you for reading "Decide."

It's time to decide to make this book done. The question might be for you (and for me):

Now what?

I'd love to hear what's next for you.

1. How did this book help you move forward?
2. Do you feel more in control of your decision-making process?
3. Is your life lighter?

We'll never be done making decisions, but each one is a small victory. Congratulations on making this one to finish this book.

Thank you, thank you, thank you for reading.

Sincerely,

Bradley

Driebergen, The Netherlands

ALSO BY BRADLEY CHARBONNEAU

Most of my books are also available as audiobooks (which I giddily narrate). Search for my name at your favorite audiobook distributor, slip on your headphones, and let me take you away.

Repossible

Who Will You Be Next?

1. Repossible
2. Every Single Day (+ Playbook)
3. Ask
4. Dare
5. Create (also available: Box Set #1)
6. Decide
7. Meditate
8. Spark (also available: Box Set #2)
9. Surrender
10. Play
11. Celebrate (also available: Box Set #3 and Box Set Complete)
12. Frequency
13. Evaluate (2022)
14. Elevate (2022)
15. Give (2022)

Create

Inspired Action to Create the Next Chapter of Your Life

1. You Don't Have To
2. How to Write Your Worst Book Ever
3. The One-Word-Long Book that Will Probably Change Your Life
4. Audio for Authors
5. Chapter Won

Charlie Holiday

The Chance is Yours

1. Now Is Your Chance
2. Second Chance
3. Chance of a Lifetime (also available: Box Set)

Short Trips

Just Put on the Shoes

1. Secret Bus to Paradise
2. Where I (Already) Am
3. Pass the Sour Cream
4. A Trip to Hel
5. Goddamn Attitude
6. Drive-By Dropping

Li & Lu

Bring Adventure Home

1. The Secret of Kite Hill
2. The Secret of Markree Castle
3. The Key to Markree Castle
4. The Gift of Markree Castle
5. Driehoek (also available: Box Set)

Really Old ...

urban travel guide SAN FRANCISCO